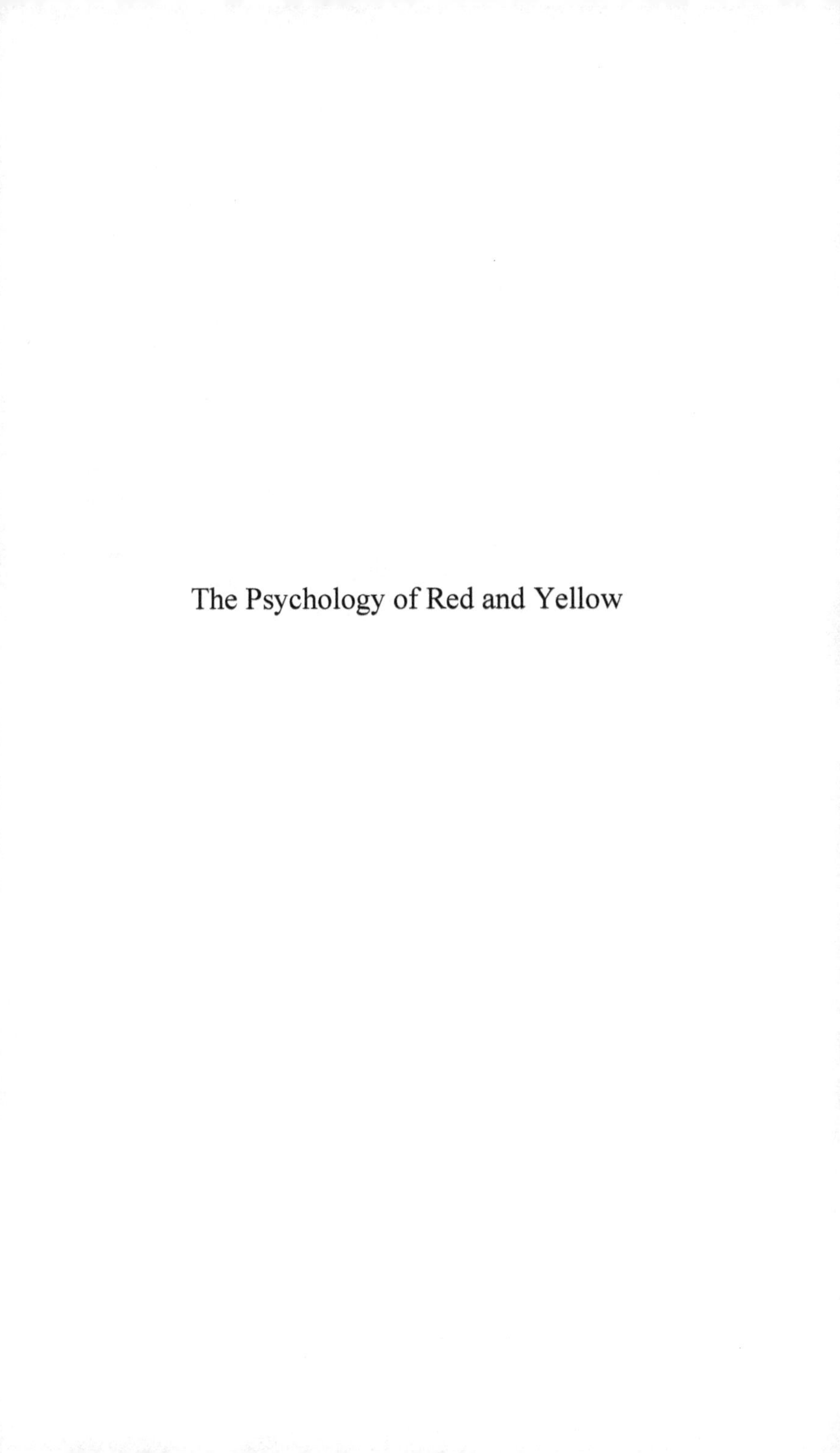

The Psychology of Red and Yellow

The Psychology of Red and Yellow

By Henry Havelock Ellis

Part I.

The Psychology of Red

I

Among all colors, the most poignantly emotional tone undoubtedly belongs to red. The ancient observation concerning the resemblance of scarlet to the notes of a trumpet has often been repeated, though it was probably unknown to the young Japanese lady who, on hearing a boy sing in a fine contralto voice, exclaimed: "That boy's voice is red." On the one hand, red is the color that idiots most easily learn to recognize; on the other hand, Kirchhoff, the chemist, called it the most aristocratic of colors; Pouchet, the zoologist, was inclined to think that it was a color apart, not to be paralleled with any other chromatic sensation, and recalled that the retinal pigment is red; Laycock, the physician, confessed that he preferred the gorgeous red tints of an autumn sunset to either musical sounds or gustatory flavors. Artists more cautious than men of science in expressing such a preference — knowing that a color possesses its special virtue in relation to other colors, and that all are of infinite variety — yet easily reveal, one may often note, a predilection for red by introducing it into scenes where it is not naturally obvious, whether we turn to a great landscape painter like Constable or to a great figure painter like Rubens, who, with the development of his genius, displayed even greater daring in the introduction of red pigments into his work.

In all parts of the world red is symbolical of joyous emotion. Often, either alone or in association with yellow, occasionally with green, it is the fortunate or sacred color. In lauds so far apart as France and Madagascar scarlet garments were at one time the exclusive privilege of the royal family. A great many different colors are symbolical of mourning in various parts of the world; white, gray, yellow, brown, blue, violet, black can be so used, but, so far as I am aware, red never. Everywhere we find, again, that red pigments and dyes, and especially red ochre, are apparently the first to be used at the beginning of civilization, and that they usually continue to be preferred even after other colors are introduced.

There is indeed one quarter of the globe where the allied color of yellow, which often elsewhere is the favorite after red, may be said to come first. In a region of which the Malay peninsula is the center and which includes a large part of China. Burmah and the lower coast of India, yellow is the sacred and preferred color, but this is the only large district which presents us with any exception to the general rule, among either higher or lower races, and since yellow falls into the same group as red, and belongs to a neighboring part of the spectrum, even this phenomenon can scarcely be said to clash seriously with the general uniformity.

If we turn to Australia, whither the anthropologist often turns in order to explore some of the most primitive and undisturbed data of early human culture still available for study, we find the preference for red very well marked. In times of rejoicing the tribes at Port Mackay, Curr remarked, paint themselves red; in times of mourning, white. In describing the paintings and rock carvings of the Australians, Mathews states that red, white, black and occasionally yellow pigments were used, precisely the four pigments which Karl von den Steinen found in use in Central Brazil. Prof. Baldwin Spencer and Mr. Gillen, in their valuable work on the natives of Central Australia, have pointed out the significance and importance of red ochre. One of the most striking and characteristic features, they say, of Central Australians' implements and weapons is the coating of red ochre with which the native covers everything except his spear and spear-thrower. The hair is greased and red-ochred, and red ochre is the most striking feature in decoration generally. For ages past the Australian native has been accustomed to rub this substance regularly over his most sacred objects, and then over ordinary objects.

There is, however, no need to go so far afield in order to illustrate the primitive use of red ochre. Our own European ancestors followed exactly the same methods, and the German woman of early ages used red and yellow ochre to adorn her face and body, while the finds of the ice age at Schussenquelle, described by Praas, included a brilliant red paste (oxide of iron with reindeer fat) evidently intended for purposes of adornment. Moreover, the early artists of classic times had precisely the same predilections in color as the aboriginal Australian artists. Red, white, black and yellow are the dominant colors in the

Iliad, and Pliny mentions that the most ancient pictures were painted in various reds, while at a later date red and yellow predominated. He also mentions that yellow was the favorite color of women for garments, and was specially used at marriages, while red being a sacred color and apt to provoke joy, was used at popular festivals, in the form of minium and cinnabar, to smear the statutes of Jupiter.

This well-nigh universal recognition of the peculiarly intense emotional tone of red is reflected in language. The color words of civilized and uncivilized peoples have been investigated with interesting and on the whole remarkably harmonious results. It is only necessary here to refer to them briefly in so far as they are related to our present subject. It seems that in every country the words for the colors at the red end of the spectrum are of earlier appearance, more definite and more numerous, than for those at the violet end. On the Niger it appears that there are only three color words, red, white and black, and everything that is not white or black is called red. The careful investigation of the natives of Torres Straits and New Guinea by Dr. W. IT. R. Rivers, of the Cambridge Anthropological Expedition, has shown that at Murray Island, Mabuiag and Kiwai there were definite names for red, less definite for yellow, still less so for green, while any definite name for blue could not be found. In this way as we pass from the colors of long wave-length towards those of short wave-length we find the color nomenclature becoming regularly less definite. In Kiwai and Murray Island the same word was applied to blue and black, and at Mabuiag there was a word (for sea-color) which could be applied either to blue or green, while Australian natives from Fitzroy River seemed limited to words for red, white and black. In a neighboring region of Northern Queensland Dr. Walter Roth has reached almost identical results, the tribes having distinct names for red and yellow, as applied to ochre, while blue is confounded in nomenclature with black.

In Brazil, again, while all tribes use separate words for red, yellow, white and black, only one had a word for blue and green. Even so æsthetic a people as the Japanese have no general words for either blue or green, and apply the same color word to a green tree and the unclouded sky.

Here again we may trace similar phenomena in Europe; the same greater primitiveness, precision and copiousness of the color vocabulary at the long wave end of the spectrum are found among Europeans as well as among the lowest savages. The vagueness of the Greek color vocabulary, especially at the violet end of the spectrum, has led to much controversy. Latin was especially rich in synonyms for red and yellow, very poor in synonyms for green and blue. The Latin tongue had even to borrow a word for blue from Teutonic speech; *caeruleus* originally meant dark. Even in the second century A. D. Aulus Gellius, who knew seven synonyms for red and yellow, scarcely mentions green and blue. Magnus has pointed out that a preference for the colors at the violet end of the spectrum coincided with the spread of Christianity, to which we owe it, he believes, that yellow ceased to be popular and was treated with opprobrium. Modern English bears witness that our ancestors, like the Homeric poets, resembled the Australian aborigines in identifying the color of the short wave end of the spectrum with entire absence of color, for 'blue' and 'black' appear to be etymologically the same word.

At this point we come across an interesting and once warmly debated question. It was maintained some twenty years ago by writers who had been impressed by the defectiveness of the color vocabulary at the short wave-length end of the spectrum, that primitive man generally, and early Hellenic man in particular, were insensitive to the colors at that end of the spectrum, and unable to distinguish them. On investigation of individuals belonging to savage races it appeared, however, that no marked inferiority in color discrimination could be demonstrated. Hence it became clear that the vague and defective vocabulary for blue and green must be due to some other cause than vague and defective perception, and that sensation and nomenclature were not sufficiently parallel to enable us to argue from one to the other.

That, in the main, is a conclusion which still holds good. In all parts of the world it has been found that color discrimination, even amongst the lowest savages, is far more accurate than color nomenclature. Thus of an African Bantu tribe, the Mang'anja, Miss Werner states that they can discriminate all varieties of blue in beads, but call them all black. The sky is black: so is any green, brown or grey article, though a very bright grey counts as white. Violet or purple is black. Yellow is either red or white. A word supposed sometimes to mean green really means raw, unripe or even wet. Thus the Mang'anja only have three colors — black, white and red.

In quite a different region, the Zulus, more advanced in color nomenclature, have not only black, white and red, but a word which may mean either green or blue, and another which means yellow, buff or grey, or some shade of brown. At the same time it now appears that the earlier scientific writers on this subject were not entirely wrong in stating that among savages there is some actual failure of perception at the short wave end of the spectrum, although they were wrong in arguing that it was necessarily involved in the defects of color vocabulary, and in imagining that it could be as extensive as that hypothesis demanded.

It now appears that the conclusions reached by Hugo Magnus of Breslau, as expressed in 1883 in his study 'Ueber Ethnologische Untersuchungen des Farbensinnes,' fairly answer to the facts. In large measure relying on the examination of 300 Chukchis made by Almquist during the Nordenskiold Expedition, Magnus concluded that although the color vision of the uncivilized has the same range from red to violet as that of the civilized and all the colors can usually be separately distinguished, there is sometimes a certain dullness, a diminished energy of sensation, as regards green and blue, the shorter and more refrangible waves of the spectrum, while the colors at the other end are perceived with much greater vividness. Stephenson, more recently, among over one thousand Chinese, examined at various places, found only one case of color blindness, but a frequent tendency to confuse green and blue and also blue and purple, while Dr. Adele Fielde, of Swatow, China, among 1,200 Chinese of both sexes examined by Thomson's wool test, found that more than half mixed up green and blue, and many even seemed to be quite blind to violet. Ernest Krause also has argued that primitive man was most sensitive to the red end of the spectrum, hence setting about to obtain red pigments and acquiring definite names for them, an explanation which is accepted by Karl von den Steinen to account for the phenomena among the Central Brazilians. The recent investigations of Rivers at Torres Straits have confirmed the conclusions of Magnus. He found that, corresponding to the defect of color terminology, though to a much less degree, there appeared to be an actual defect of vision for colors of short wave-length; in testing with colored wools no mistake was ever made with reds, but blues and greens were constantly confused, as were blue and violet.

It may even be argued that the same defect exists to a minor degree not only among the peoples of Eastern Asia whose æsthetic sense is highly developed, but among civilized Europeans when any kind of color blindness is altogether excluded. This was noted long since by Holmgren, who remarked that some persons, though able to distinguish between blue and green wools when placed together, were liable to call the blue wool green, and the green blue, when they saw them separately. Magnus also showed that such an inability is apt to appear at a very early stage in some persons when the illumination is diminished, although the perception of red and yellow remains perfectly distinct. He further showed that blue and green at certain distances are often much more difficult to recognize than red. Most people probably are conscious of difficulty in distinguishing blue and green pigments with diminished light and find that blue easily passes into black. Violet also appears for many people to be merely a variety of blue; the word itself, we may note, is recent in our language, and plays a very small part in our poetic literature, and in fact the color itself, if we rigidly exclude purple, is extremely rare in nature. It is a noteworthy fact in this connection that in normal persons the color sense may be easily educated; this is not merely a fact of daily observation, but has been exactly demonstrated by Féré, who by means of his chromoptoscopic boxes, containing very dilute colored solutions, found that with practice it was possible to recognize solutions which had previously seemed uncolored. It is also noteworthy that in the achromatopsia of the hysterical, as Charcot showed and as Parimand has since confirmed, the order in which the colors usually disappear is violet, green, blue, red; sometimes the paradoxical fact is found that red will give a luminous sensation in a contracted visual field when even white gives no luminous sensation. This persistence of red vision in the hysterical is only one instance of a predilection for red which has often been noted as very marked among the hysterical. Red also exerted a great fascination over the victims of the mediæval hysterical epidemics of tarantism in Italy, while the victims of the German mediæval epidemic of St. Vitus's dance imagined that they were immersed in a stream of blood which compelled them to leap up.

It may be noted that red and perhaps yellow have been stated to be the only colors visible in dreams; this is possibly due to the blood-vessels. Such an explanation is probable with regard to the various subjective visual sensations which constitute an aura in epilepsy, among which, as Gowers notes, red and reddish yellow are most frequently found. Féré has further noted that in various emotional states somewhat resembling epilepsy, and even in mystic exaltation, red may be subjectively seen. Simroth has gone so far as to argue that not only is red fundamental in human color psychology, but that in living organisms generally, even as a pigment, red is the most primitive of colors, that since the algae at the greatest sea-depths are red it is possible that protoplasm at first only responded to rays of long wave-length, and that with increased metabolism colors became differentiated, following the order in the spectrum.

If it is really the case that in the evolution of the race familiarity with the red end of the spectrum has been earlier and more perfectly acquired than with the violet end, and that red and yellow made a more profound impression on primitive man than green and blue, we should expect to find this evolution reflected in the development of the individual, and that the child would earlier acquire a sensitiveness for red and orange and yellow than for green and blue and violet. This seems actually to be the case. The study of the color sense in children is, indeed, even more difficult than in savages; and many investigators have probably succumbed to the fallacies involved in this study. Doubtless we may thus account for some discrepancies in the attempts to ascertain the facts of color perception and color preference in children, while doubtless also there are individual differences which discount the value of experiments made on only a single child. A few careful and elaborate investigations, however, especially that of Garbini on 600 North Italian children of various ages, have thrown much light on the matter. There is fairly general agreement that red is the first color that attracts young children and which they recognize. That is the result recorded by Uffelmann in Germany, while Preyer found yellow and red at the head; Binet in France concluded that red comes first; Wolfe in America reached the same result, and Luckey noted that his own children seemed to enjoy red, orange and yellow very much earlier than they could perceive blue, which seemed to come last. Baldwin, indeed, found in the case of his own child that blue seemed more attractive than red; his methods have, however, been criticised, and his experiments failed to include yellow. Mrs. Moore found that her baby, between the sixteenth and forty-fifth weeks, nearly always preferred a yellow ball to a red ball; this was doubtless not a matter of color, but of brightness, for there is no reason to suppose chromatic perception at so early an age. Red, orange and yellow, it may be added, are perceived by a slightly lower illumination than green, blue and violet, the last being the most difficult of all to perceive, so that it is not surprising that the colors at the violet end should be inconspicuous to young infants. Garbini, whose experiments are worth noting in more detail, found that the order of perception is red, green, yellow, orange, blue and violet, and as he experimented with a large number of children and used methods which so competent a judge as Binet regards as approaching perfection, his results may be considered a fair approach to the truth. He found that for the first few days after birth the infant shuns the light; then, about the fourteenth day, he ceases to be photophobic and begins to enjoy the light, as is shown by his being quieted when brought into a bright light and crying when taken from it; this may sometimes begin even about the fifth day. Between the fifth week and the eighteenth month children show signs of distinguishing white, black and grey objects. It is not until after the eighteenth month that their chromatic perception begins, any preference for red and yellow objects at an earlier age being due merely to their greater luminosity. Garbini considers that it is the center of the retina, or the portion most sensitive to red and yellow, which is most exercised in young infants. Between the second and third years children, both boys and girls, were found to be most successful in the recognition of red, then of green, but they very often confused orange with red, and mixed up yellow, blue, violet and green; he thinks they tend to confuse a color with the preceding color in spectral order. Under the age of three children may be said to be color-blind, and they are liable to confuse rosy tints with green. Between the ages of three and five they are able to distinguish red in any gradation, green nearly always, with an occasional confusion with red, while yellow is sometimes confused with orange, orange sometimes replaced by rose, blue often not recognized in its gradations, and violet often selected in place of blue. At this age, also (as in hysterical anæsthesia of the retina), blue seems dark or black. In the fifth and sixth years red, green and yellow are always correctly chosen; orange gradations are not always recognized, and blue and violet come last, being sometimes confused. In the sixth year children are perfecting their knowledge of orange, blue and violet and completing their knowledge of color designations. Garbini has reached the important result that color perceptions an.d verbal expression of the perceptions follow exactly parallel paths, so that in studying verbal expression we are really studying perception, with the important distinction that the expression comes much later than the perception. These investigations of Garbini are very significant, and there can be little doubt that the evolution of the child's color sense repeats that of the race.

In dealing with the color perceptions of savages and children we are, of course, to some extent dealing more or less unconsciously with their color preferences. There is some interest from our present point of view in considering the conscious color preferences of young and adult civilized persons. Red, as we have seen, is the color that fascinates our attention earliest, that we see and recognize most vividly; it remains the color that attracts our attention most readily and that gives us the greatest emotional shock. It by no means necessarily follows that it is the most pleasurable color. As a matter of fact, such evidence as is available shows that very often it is not. There seems reason to think that after the first early perception of red, and early pleasure in it, yellow or orange is frequently the favorite color, the preference often lasting during several years of childhood; Preyer's child liked and discriminated yellow best, and Miss Shinn was inclined to think that it was the favorite color of her niece, who in the twenty-eighth month showed a special fondness for daffodils and for a yellow dress. Barnes found that in children the love of yellow diminishes with age. Binet's child was specially preoccupied with orange. Aars in an elaborate and frequently varied investigation into the color preferences of eight children (four of each sex), between four and seven years of age, found that with the boys the order of preference was blue and yellow (both equal), then red, lastly green; while with the girls the order was green, blue, red and yellow; in combinations of two colors it was found that combinations of blue come first, then of yellow, then green, lastly red. It was found (as J. Cohn has found among adults and cultivated people) that the deepest and most saturated color was most pleasing; and also that the love of novelty and of variety was an important factor. It will be observed that at this age green was the girls' favorite color and that least liked by the boys, whose favorite color, in combination, was blue; the number of individuals was, however, small. This was in Germany. In America, among 1,000 children, probably somewhat older on the average (though I have not details of the inquiry), Mr. Earl Barnes found, like Dr. Aars, that more boys than girls selected blue, while the girls preferred red more frequently than the boys; Barnes considers that with growing years there is a growing tendency to select red; as is well known, girls are more precocious than boys. Among 100 students at Columbia University, the order of preference was found to be blue (34 per cent), red (22.7 per cent), and then at a more considerable distance violet, yellow, green. It is noteworthy that among 100 women students at Wellesley College the order of preference was not very different, being blue (38 per cent), red (18 per cent), yellow, green, violet; in a later investigation the order remained the same, there being only some increase in the preference for red; it was considered that association accounted for the preference for blue, while more conscious as well as more emotional elements entered into the preference for red.

By far the most extensive investigation of color preference was that carried on at Chicago by Professor Jastrow on 4,500 persons, mostly adults, of both sexes and various nationalities.

Blue was found to be the favorite color, less than half as many persons preferring red; of every thirty men ten voted for blue and three for red, while of every thirty women five voted for red and four for blue. The men also liked violet and on the whole confined their choice to but few colors, the women also liked pink, green (very seldom chosen by men) and yellow, and showed a tendency to choose light and dainty shades. There was on the whole a decided preference for dark shades; the least favorite colors were yellow and orange. It is evident that, as we should expect, within the elementary field of popular esthetics, women show a more trained feeling for color than men.

It is not quite easy to coördinate the various phenomena of color predilection. Careful and extended observations are still required. It seems to me, however, that the facts, as at present ascertained, do suggest a certain order and harmony in the phenomena. It is difficult not to believe that there really is, both among many uncivilized peoples and also many children at an early age, even to a slight extent among civilized adults, a relative inability, by no means usually absolute, to recognize and distinguish the tones of color at the more refrangible end of the spectrum. The earliest writers on the subject were wrong when they supposed that color nomenclature at all accurately corresponded to color perception, and it is well recognized that there are no peoples who are wholly unable to distinguish between green and blue and black. But as Garbini has clearly shown, there really is a parallelism between color nomenclature and color recognition, and Garbini's wide investigation has confirmed the experiments of Preyer on a single child by showing that there is a certain hesitancy and uncertainty in recognizing the colors at the more refrangible end of the spectrum, long after children are familiar with the less refrangible end. In the same way the important investigations of Rivers have confirmed the earlier observations of Magnus and Almquist in showing that savages in many cases exhibit a certain difficulty in recognizing and distinguishing blue and green, such as they never experience with red and yellow. The ness of color nomenclature as regards blue and green thus indicates, though grossly exaggerating, a real psychological fact, and in this way we have an explanation of the curious fact that in widely separated parts of the world (at Torres Straits, among the Esthonians at Rome, etc.) as civilization progressed it was found necessary to borrow a word for blue from other languages.

There is almost complete harmony among a number of observers, now very considerable, in many countries, showing that the colors children first take notice of and recognize are red and yellow, most observers putting red first. There is no true predilection for these colors at this early age because the other colors do not yet seem to have been perceived. At first, doubtless, all colors appear to the infant as light or dark, white or black. That this is so is indicated by the experience of Dr. George Harley, who at one period of his life, in order to cure an injury to the retina caused by overwork at the microscope, resolutely spent nine months in absolutely total and uninterrupted darkness. When he emerged he found that, like an infant, he was unable to appreciate distance by the eye, while he had also lost the power of recognizing colors; for the first month all light colors appeared to him perfectly white and all dark colors perfectly black. He fails to state the order in which the colors reappeared to him. It is well recognized, however, that eyes long unexposed to light become color-blind for all colors except red. Preyer's child in the fourth year was surprised that in the twilight her bright blue stockings looked grey, while for some time longer she always called dark green black. By the sixth year all colors are seen and known with fair correctness. Among young children at this age, so far as the evidence yet goes, red is rarely the preferred color, this being more often yellow, green or blue. There is doubtless room here for a great amount of individual difference, but on the whole it appears that children prefer those colors which they have most recently learnt to recognize, the colors which have all the charm of novelty and newly-won possession. It is probable, too, that (as Groos has also suggested) the stimulation of red is too painfully strong in this stage of the development of the color sense to be altogether pleasurable, in the same way that orchestral music is often only a disturbing noise to children.

One may note in this connection that hyperesthesia to color is nearly always an undue sensibility to red and very rarely to any other color. The case has been recorded of a highly neurotic officer who, for more than thirty years, was intolerant of red-colored objects. The dazzling produced by scarlet uniforms, especially in bright sunshine, seriously interfered with the performance of his duties, and in private life red parasols, shawls, etc., produced similar effects; he was often overcome in the streets by giddiness, sometimes almost before he realized that he was looking at a red object. Many years ago Laycock referred to the case of a lady who could not hear to look at anything red, and Elliston also had a lady patient to whom red was very obnoxious, and who, when put into a room with red curtains, drank seven quarts of fluid a day. I am not aware that any such hyperæsthesia exists in the case of other colors. It is also noteworthy that the morbid affection in which color is seen when it does not exist is most usually a condition in which red is seen (erythropsia), yellow being the color most frequently seen after red (a condition called xanthopsia); the other colors are very rarely seen, and Hilbert, in his monograph on the pathology of the color sense, considers that this is due to the fact that red and yellow make the most intense effect on the sensorium, which thus becomes liable not only to direct but to reflected irritation, in the absence of any external color stimulus. There are other facts which show that of all colors red is that which acts as the most powerful stimulus on the organism.

Münsterberg, in some interesting experiments which he made to illustrate the motor power of visual impressions as measured by their arresting action on the eye-muscles, found that red and yellow have considerably more motor power in stimulating the eye than the other colors. It may be added also that, as Quantz has found, we overestimate the magnitude of colors of the less refrangible part of the spectrum and underestimate the others.

After puberty blue seems still to maintain its position, but red has now come more to the front, while yellow has definitely receded; although so favorite a color in classic antiquity, it is rarely the preferred color among ourselves. J. Cohn in Germany found that among a dozen students it was never in any degree of saturation the preferred color, while at Cornell Major found that all the subjects investigated considered yellow and orange either unpleasant or among the least pleasant colors.

While blue seems to be the color most usually preferred by men, red is more commonly preferred by women, who also show a more marked predilection for its complementary green. Whether the feminine love of red shows a fine judgment we could better decide if we knew among what classes of the population red lovers and blue lovers respectively predominate; it may be noted, however, that the necessities of dress give the most ordinary woman an acquaintance with the elementary æsthetics of color which the average man has no occasion to acquire. In any case it might have been anticipated that, even though the typically 'cold' color should appeal most strongly to men, the most emotional of colors should appeal most strongly to women.

II

The facts and considerations we have passed in review fairly indicate the physiological and psychological preëminence of red among the colors of the spectrum to which we are sensitive. What is the cause of that preëminence?

It seems to me that two orders of causes have coöperated to produce this predominant influence, one physical and depending on the special effects of the long-waved portion of the spectrum on living matter, the other psychological and resulting from the special environmental influences to which man, and to some extent even the higher animals generally, have been subjected.

It is possible that these two influences blend together and cannot at any point be disentangled; it is possible that acquired aptitude may be inherited or that what seem to be acquired aptitudes are really perpetuated congenital variations; but on the whole the two influences are so distinct that we may deal with them separately.

On the physical side the influence of the red rays, although there is much evidence showing that it may be traced throughout the whole of organic nature, is certainly most strongly and convincingly exhibited on plants. The characteristic greenness of vegetation alone bears witness to this fact. The red rays are life to the chlorophyll-bearing plant, the violet rays are death. A meadow, it has been justly said, is a vast field of tongues of fire greedily licking up the red rays and vomiting forth the poisonous bile of blue and yellow. An experiment of Flammarion's has beautifully shown the widely different reaction of plants to the red and violet rays.

At the climatological station at Juvisy he constructed four greenhouses — one of ordinary transparent glass, another of red glass, another of green, the fourth of dark blue. The glass was monochromatic, as carefully tested by the spectroscope, and dark blue was used instead of violet because it was impossible to obtain a perfect violet glass. These were all placed under uniform meteorological and other conditions, and from certain plants such as the sensitive plant, previously sown on the same day in the same soil, eight of each kind were selected, all measuring 27 millimetres, and placed by two and two in the four greenhouses on the 4th of July. On the 15th of August there were notable differences in height, color and sensitiveness, and these differences continued to become marked; photographs of the plants on the 4th of October showed that while those under blue glass had made no progress, those under red glass had attained extraordinary development, red light acting like a manure. While those under blue glass became insensitive, under red glass the sensitive plants had become excessively sensitive to the least breath. They also flowered, those under transparent glass being vigorous and showing buds, but not flowering. The foliage under red glass was very light, under blue darkest. Similar but less marked effects were found in the case of geraniums, strawberries, etc. The strawberries under blue glass were no more advanced in October than in May; though not growing old their life was little more than a sleep. It appears, however, that the stimulating influence of red light fails to influence favorably the ripening of fruit. Zacharewiez, professor of agriculture at Vaucluse, has found that red, or rather orange, produces the greatest amount of vegetation, while as regards fruit, the finest and earliest was grown under clear glass, violet glass, indeed, causing the amount of fruit to increase but at the expense of the quality.

Moreover, the lowest as well as the highest plants participated in this response to the red rays, and in even a more marked degree, for they perish altogether under the influence of the violet rays. Marshall Ward and others have shown that the blue, violet and ultra-violet rays, but no others, are deleterious to bacteria. Finsen has successfully made use of this fact in the treatment of bacterial skin diseases.

Reynolds Green has shown that while the ultra-violet rays have a destructive influence on diastase, the red rays have a powerfully stimulating effect, increasing diastase and converting zymogen into diastase.

While the influence of the red rays on the plant is thus so enormous and easily demonstrated, the physical effects of red on animals seem to be even opposite in character, although results of experiments are somewhat contradictory. Béclard found that the larva? of the flesh fly raised under violet glass were three fourths larger than those raised under green glass; the order was violet, blue, red, yellow, white, green. In the case of tadpoles, Yung found that violet or blue was especially favorable to the growth of frogs; he also found that fish hatch most rapidly under violet light. Thus the influence that is practically death to plants is that most favorable to life in animals. Both effects, however, as Davenport truly remarks in his 'Experimental Morphology,' when summing up the results of investigations, are due to the same chemical metabolic changes, but while plants succumb to the influence of the violet rays, animals, being more highly organized, are able to take advantage of them and flourish.

At the same time the influence of violet rays on animal tissue is by no means invariably beneficial; they are often too powerful a stimulant. That the violet rays have an influence on the human skin which in the first place, at all events, is destructive and harmful in a high degree, is now clearly established by the observations and experiments of Charcot, Unna, Hammer, Bowles and others, while Finsen has made an important advance in the treatment of disease based on this fact. The conditions called 'sun-burn,' 'snow-burn' 'snow-blindness' for instance, which may affect even travelers on snow-fields and Arctic explorers, are now known to be wholly due to the violet and not to the red rays. Unna's device of wearing a yellow veil, and Bowles's plan of painting the skin brown, thus shutting off the violet rays, suffice to prevent sunburn. The same effect is also obtained by nature, which under the stress of sunlight, and largely through the irritation of the violet rays themselves, weaves a pigmentary veil of yellow and brown on the skin, which thus protects from the further injurious influence of the violet rays and renders the sunlight a source of less alloyed joy and health.

That the presence of the red rays, or at all events the exclusion of the violet, is of great benefit in many skin diseases seems to be now beyond doubt. This has been shown by Finsen in his treatment of smallpox in red rooms; it appears that it was also known in the Middle Ages as well as in Japan, Tonquin and Roumania, red bed-covers, curtains or carpets being used to obtain the effect. Under the treatment by red light not only is the skin enabled to heal healthfully without scarring, but the whole course of the disease is beneficially affected and abbreviated, the fever is diminished and also the risk of complications. Another physician has discovered that a similar beneficial effect is produced by red light in measles. A child with a severe attack of measles was put into a room with red blinds and a photographic lamp. The rash speedily disappeared and the fever subsided, the child complaining only of the absence of light; the blinds were consequently removed, and the fever, rash and prostration returned, to disappear again when the blinds were resumed.

Whether red light, or the exclusion of violet, exerts a beneficial influence on the hæmoglobin of the blood and on metabolism generally has not been distinctly proved, but it seems to me to be indicated by such experiments as those of Marti published a few years ago in the *Atti del Lincei*. This investigator found that while feeble irritation of the skin promotes the formation of blood corpuscles, strong irritation diminishes the blood corpuscles and also the hæmoglobin; at the same time he found that darkness also diminishes the number of red corpuscles, while continued exposure to intense light (even at night the electric light, which, however, is rich in violet rays) favors increased formation of red corpuscles, and in some degree of haemoglobin. Finsen has shown that inflammation of the skin caused by chemical or violet light leads to contraction of the red corpuscles.

This brings us to the consideration of the influence of the red rays on the nervous system. From time to time experiments have been made as to the influence of various colored lights, chiefly on the insane, as first suggested by Father Secchi in 1895. Even yet, however, the specific mental influences of the various colors are not quite clear. It has been found by some that the red rays are far more soothing and comfortable, less irritating, than the total rays of uncolored light, and Garbini found that angry infants were soothed by the light through red glass, only slightly by that through green and not at all by other colored light. On the other hand, it is stated that a well-known dry plate manufacturer at Lyons was obliged to substitute green-colored glass in the windows of his large room for the usual red because the work people sang and gesticulated all day and the men made love to the women, while under the influence of green glass (which also allows yellow rays to pass) they became quiet and silent and seemed less fatigued when they left off work.

We need not attach much value to these statements, but in this connection it is interesting to refer to the results obtained some years ago by Féré and recorded in his *'Sensation et Mouvement.'* Experimenting on normal subjects as well as on nervous subjects, who were found more sensitive, with colored light passed through glass or sheets of gelatine, he found notable differences in muscular power, measured by the dynamometer, and in the circulation as measured by plethysmography tracings of the forearm under the influence of different colors. He found in this manner with one subject whose normal muscular power was represented by 23 that blue light increased his power to 24, green to 28, yellow to 30, orange to 35 and red to 42. The dynamogenic powers of the different colors were thus found to rank in the spectral order, red representing the climax of energy, or, as Féré puts it, "the intensity of the visual sensation varies as the vibrations." Féré found that colors need not be perceived in order to show their influence, thus proving the purely physical nature of that influence, for in a subject who was unable to see colors with one eye, the color stimulus had the same dynamogenic effect whether applied to the seeing or the defective eye. Increase of volume of blood in the limbs, measured by the plethysmograph, so far as we can rely on Féré's experiments, ran parallel with the influence on muscular power, culminating with red, so that no metaphor is involved, Féré remarks, when we speak of red as a 'warm' color. On the insane the results attained by the use of colored glass do not seem to be quite coherent. Some of the earlier observers described the beneficial effects of blue glass in soothing maniacs. Pritchard Davies, however, was not able to find that red light had any beneficial effect, though on some cases blue had, while Roffegean found that, in the case of a somber and taciturn maniac who could rarely be persuaded to eat, three hours in a red-lighted room produced a markedly beneficial effect, and a man with delusions of persecution became quite rational and was even in a condition to be sent home after a few days in the same room. He also found that a violent maniac wearing a strait jacket, after a few hours in a room with blue glass windows became quite calm and gave no further trouble. Osburne has found, after many years' experience, that in the absence of structural disease violet light (for from three to six hours) is most useful in the treatment of excitement, sleeplessness and acute mania; red he has found of some benefit, though to a much less degree in such cases (it must be remarked that violet light as usually applied is not free from red), while he has not found any color with which he has tried experiments (red, orange or violet) of benefit in melancholia. The significance of these facts is not altogether clear; the influence, as Pritchard Davies concluded, seems to be largely moral, though it may be that the colors of long wave-length are tonic and those of short wave-length sedative.

So far I have been chiefly concerned to point out that the immense emotional impressiveness of red has a basis in physical laws, being by no means altogether a matter of environmental associations. It is true that the two groups of influences overlap, and that we can not always distinguish them. We can not be sure that the greater sensitiveness to the red rays may not have been emphasized in the organism, not necessarily as the result of inherited acquirement, but probably as the perpetuation of a variation of sensibility, found beneficial in an environment where red was liable to be especially associated with objects that were to be avoided as terrible or sought as useful. In this way the physical and environmental factors would run in a circle.

We have to bear this consideration in mind when we take into account the susceptibilities of animals, especially of the higher animals, to red. The color sense, it is well known, is widely diffused among animals; indeed this fact has been brought forward, especially by Pouchet, to prove that there can have been no color evolution in man; this it can scarcely be said to show, since evolution does not run in a straight line, and it is quite conceivable and even probable that the ancestors of man were less dependent than many lower animals, for the means of living, on a highly developed color sense. Thus a color sense that among some creatures is so highly developed as to include even the ultra-violet rays, was among our own ape-like ancestors either never developed or partially lost.

Graber, in his important investigation into the color sense of animals, showed that of fifty animals studied by him forty showed strong color preferences in their places of abode. In general he found, without being able to explain the fact, that animals which prefer the dark are red lovers, those which prefer the light are blue lovers. The common worm, with head and tail cut off, still preferred red to blue nearly as much as when uninjured. (This would seem to indicate the same kind of susceptibility to unaccustomed violet rays which we have already encountered in the phenomenon of sunburn.) The triton and cochineal, with eyes removed and heads covered with wax, still had delicate sense for color and brightness. The flea infesting the dog had a finer color sense than the bee, while nearly all the animals Graber investigated were more or less sensitive to the ultra-red rays.

Among insects it scarcely appears, nor should we expect that there would be any peculiarly marked predilection or aversion for red. Cockerell and F. W. Anderson, from observations in various parts of the United States, believe that yellow (*i. e.,* the brightest color) is the most attractive to insects, and the former doubts whether insects can distinguish red from yellow. Among the higher animals, and even among fishes and birds, there is not only a color sense, but a highly emotionalized color sense, and red appears to be usually the color that arouses the emotion. There is a proverb, 'Women and mackerel are caught by red,' and perch is also said to be caught by red bait. Sparrows appear to be repelled by red; the case is reported of a hen sparrow, kept in captivity for ten years, which though otherwise a fearless bird 'would on seeing scarlet show painful signs of distress and faint away.' The lady who records this observation has noted the same repugnance to red, though in a less marked degree, in other sparrows, one of which showed a predilection for blue objects, and she remarks that when feeding outdoor sparrows from the window they flew away when she wore a red jacket, while a blue jacket inspired them with confidence; other birds, she found, except a cockatoo, were unaffected by colors. Red, it is well known, is very obnoxious to turkey cocks, while the fury aroused in various quadrupeds by red was known at a very early period; Seneca referred to it in the case of the bull, the most familiar example; it is seen in buffaloes, sometimes in horses, and also, it is said, in the hippopotamus.

The phenomena of color aversion and color predilection among insects may possibly be in some degree a matter of physical sensibility, varying according to the creature's tissues, habitat and needs, but as we approach the vertebrates and especially the mammals there can be little doubt that it is mainly a matter of environment and association; in other words, that it is accounted for by the color of food, the color of blood and the color of the chief secondary sexual characters.

Let us, however, confine ourselves to man, and consider what are the chief colored objects that are of most vital concern to the human and most closely allied species.

One of the earliest groups of such objects—some would say the most important group in this connection—is that of ripe fruits. Certainly among the frugivorous apes and among many races of primitive man, the color of fruits must be a powerful factor in developing a sensibility for red rays, and in associating such sensibility with emotional satisfaction. The color of fruits is most generally red, orange or purple, and since purple is largely made up of red, it is clear that the influence of fruits will almost exclusively bear on the rays of long wave-length. We may reasonably suppose that the search for fruits acted as an important factor in the development of a special sensibility for red.

A later factor in the predilection for the red, orange and yellow rays, though scarcely a factor in their discrimination, lies in the fact that these are the colors of fire. Flame, apart from its beauty, on which certain poets, Shelley especially, have often insisted, is a source of massive physical satisfaction. Even under the conditions of civilization we are often acutely sensitive to this fact, while under the conditions of primitive life, in imperfect shelters, caves or tents, where no other source of artificial light and heat is known, the satisfaction is immensely greater. At the same time fire is associated with food, it is a protection from wild beasts and the accompaniment of the festival. It may even take on a sacred and symbolic character, and the Roman goddess Vesta was, as Ovid said, simply 'living flame.'

While fruit or fire would tend to make the emotional tone of red pleasant, another very powerful factor in its emotional influences, though this time as much by causing terror as pleasure, is the fact that it is the color of blood. That 'the blood is the life' is a belief instinctively stamped even on the emotions of animals, and it has not died even in civilized man, for the sight of blood produces on many persons a sickening and terrifying sensation which is only overcome by habit and experience or by a very strong effort of will. It is not surprising that in some parts of the world, and even in our own Indo-European group of languages, the name for red is 'blood-color.'

It is evident, however, that at a very early period of primitive culture the blood had ceased to be merely a source of terror, or even of the joy of battle. We find everywhere that blood is blended into complex ritual customs, and thus associated with complex emotional states. Among the ancient Arabians blood was smeared on the body on various occasions, and in modern Arabia blood is still so used. Everywhere, even in the folk-lore of modern Europe, we find that blood is a medicine, as it is also among the primitive aborigines of Australia, so carefully investigated by Baldwin Spencer and Gillen. Among these latter primitive people we meet with a phenomenon of very great significance. We find, that is, that blood is the earliest pigment. There can be little doubt that the earliest paint used by man — no doubt by man when in a much more primitive condition than even the Australians — was blood. In the initiation rites of the Arunta tribes, as described by Spencer and Gillen, the chief performer is elaborately decorated with patterns in eagle-hawk down stuck to his body with blood drawn from some member of the tribe. It was estimated that one man alone, on one of these occasions, allowed five half-pints to be taken from him during a single day; at the same time the blood is not regarded as sufficient pigment and the down is also colored red and yellow with ochre. Red ochre, Spencer and Gillen remark, is frequently a substitute for blood or is used with it. Blood is a medicine, and when any one is ill he is first rubbed over with red ochre, it being obvious to the primitive mind that the ochre will share the remedial properties of blood; in the same way ceremonial objects may sometimes be rubbed over with ochre instead of blood. They associate this red ochre especially with women's blood; and it is said that once some women after long walking were so exhausted that hemorrhage came on and this gave rise to deposits of red ochre. Other red ochre pits, also, they attribute to blood which flowed from women. It appears also that the blood with which sacred implements used in the ritual ceremonies of these Central Australians were smeared must be drawn from women.

Far from Australia, among the hill tribes of the Central Indian hills, we find the same blood ritual and the same tendency to substitute pigments for blood. Among some of the Bengal tribes, says Crooke, blood is drawn from the husband's little finger, mixed with betel and eaten by the bride. A further stage is seen among the allied Kurmis who mix the blood with lac dye. Lastly come the rites, common to all these tribes, in which the bridegroom, often in secrecy, covered by a sheet, rubs vermilion on the parting of the girl's hair, while the women relations smear their toes with lac dye. It is a sacramental rite, and after the husband's death the widow solemnly washes off the red from her hair, or flings the little box in which she keeps the coloring matter into running water.

Some of the foregoing facts, both in Australia and India, suggest the transition to another factor in the emotional potency possessed by red. Red is not only the color of fire and of war and of ritual pigment; it is the color of love. This is certainly an ancient and powerful factor in the emotional attitude towards red. Secondary sexual characters, even among birds, are often red; many fishes, also, at the epoch of the oviposit show a red tint on the orifice of the sexual apparatus; patches of red, sometimes very brilliant, but only appearing when the animal is mature, are perhaps the commonest adornments of monkeys. In man the color of the hair and beard, the most conspicuous of the secondary sexual characters, is most usually brown, or some other variety of red. The lips are crimson, the mucous membrane generally a dark red; the scarlet of the blush, among all fair races, whatever other sources it may have, is always regarded as especially the ensign of love. The rose is the flower of love, as the pale lily is of virtue. This association is quite inapt, and many people who are sensitive in such matters feel that the lily and many white flowers are far more symbolical of rapture and voluptuousness than the rose. It is, however, the color and not the scent or other qualities that has exerted decisive influence on the choice of the symbol. In the Teutonic symbolism of fourteenth century Europe red was the color of love, as also, with yellow, it was the favorite color for garments. In more modern times this last tendency has survived. Sardou decides, it is reported, the color of the dresses to be worn in his plays, on the ground that if he did not the actresses would all wear red to attract attention to themselves, as once occurred at the Odéon. Eighteen hundred years earlier, Clement of Alexandria had written: "Would it were possible to abolish purple in dress, so as not to turn the eyes of the spectators on the faces of those that wear it!" He proceeds to lament that women make all their garments of purple (the classic purple was really a red) in order to inflame lust—those 'stupid and luxurious purples' which have caused Tyre and Sidon and the Lacedæmonian Sea to be so much in demand for their purple fishes. Similar phenomena are noted on the other side of the world. Thus the Japanese, as the Rev. Walter Weston informs us, have a proverb: 'Love flies with a red petticoat.' Married women are not there supposed to wear red petticoats, for they are too attractive, and a married woman should be attractive only to her husband. The æsthetic Japanese may be thought to be specially sensitive to color, but in Africa also, in Loango, as Pechuel-Loesche mentions, pregnant women are forbidden to wear red, and it would doubtless be possible to find many similar indications of this feeling in other parts of the world.

We have now passed in review all the influences which, by force of their powerful attraction or repulsion, have during countless ages impressed on man, and often on his ancestors, the strong and poignant emotions which accompany the sensation of the most vividly and persistently seen of all colors. We find evidence of the reality of the influences we have traced — especially those of fire, blood and love — in Christian ecclesiastical symbolism, according to which red variously signifies ardent love, burning zeal, energy, courage, cruelty and bloodthirstiness. To the antagonism and complexity of these influences we must doubtless attribute the disturbing nature of the emotion aroused by the group of red sensations and the fluctuations in the predilection felt towards it. It is at once the most attractive and the most repulsive of colors. To enjoy it we must use it economically. The vision of poppies on a background of golden corn, the glint of roses embowered in green leaves, the sudden flash of a scarlet flower on a southern woman's dark hair — it is in such visions as these that red gives us its emotional thrill altogether untouched by pain. If the 'multitudinous seas' were indeed 'incarnadined' for us in 'one red/ if the sky were scarlet, or all vegetation crimson, the horror of the world would be painful to contemplate for nervous systems moulded to our vision of nature. Our eyes have developed in a world where the green and blue rays meet us at every step, and where we have in consequence been almost as dulled to them as we are to the weight of the atmosphere that presses in on us on every side. It is under the clouded skies of northern lands that blue is counted the loveliest of colors; it is in the desert that green becomes supremely beautiful and sacred.

Part II
The Psychology of Yellow.

The part played by red as a powerful stimulant in the psychic life is clearly pronounced and fairly uniform among all peoples at all grades of civilization. The special emotional tone of yellow is by no means so easy to define. It varies to a marked extent at different historical periods, in different regions of the globe, even under civilized conditions, at different ages in the same individual. There is no color which is sometimes so exalted in human estimation and sometimes so debased. The psychology of yellow thus presents problems which are peculiarly difficult to unravel.

Among primitive peoples the delight in yellow seems to be almost universal. Red is the favorite color of savages, but—as in the personal decoration with ochre of the tribes of Central Australia, according to Spencer and Gillen — yellow is easily second, and sometimes perhaps on the same level with red. Indeed, it may even at times seem to be preferred to red. Thus in some parts of New Guinea, although the natives are fond of scarlet, they take the trouble to feed a certain parrot having red tail-feathers on a yellow root (for they have no means of dyeing) until the tail feathers turn yellow. As a general rule, when dyes are known, bright yellow, after or with scarlet, is the favorite color, as it was among the Society Islanders. It was so, not only among the savages of the Pacific, but also among our own ancestors, and the primitive German woman used yellow and red ochre to adorn her face and body.

The early Europeans seem to have been by no means always careful to distinguish between their two favorite colors of red and yellow; they saw both colors in gold, the most precious material of their adornments; the phrase 'red gold' is almost modern, and the Kirins of the Caucasus, according to Abercrombie, used for gold a word (borrowed from the Tartars), which also means red.

Young children, who are at one with savages at so many points, share their love of yellow, and usually indeed prefer it to red, though some writers, like Scripture, are inclined to account for this as due entirely, as in large measure it doubtless is, to the greater brightness of yellow. As to the reality of the preference among the children of various nations there seems to be little doubt. Preyer's child liked and discriminated yellow. Miss Shinn found that yellow was her niece's first favorite color, and, in her twenty-eighth month, she had a special fondness for daffodils and for a yellow gown. Mrs. Moore found that in the sixteenth week her child chose a yellow ball in preference to a red, and, later, in the forty-fifth week, six times out of ten preferred the yellow ball. Binet's child could not readily distinguish yellow, but was especially successful with orange.

A lady who made some experiments for me with a Belgian child one year of age found that when successively offered a red poppy and a yellow poppy, then red, white and yellow poppies, finally red, white, orange and yellow poppies, she on all three occasions chose the yellow poppy, though on the third trial she hesitated between the orange and the yellow poppies; when she passed yellow poppies growing she would point to them and want them, and was also observed to contemplate admiringly a sunflower, though usually indifferent to flowers of other colors, except pink geraniums. At this age, no doubt, the preference for yellow is mainly a question of luminosity, for the careful investigations of Garbini on a large number of children showed that under the age of three they may almost be described as color-blind and experience a special difficulty in distinguishing yellow, which even at a somewhat later age is often confused with orange. When children show genuine color preferences, they appear, like adults, to be only to a slight degree attracted by brilliancy, but to a large extent by depth of saturation. This was found to be the case by Aars, who in testing color preferences used colored papers of similar brilliancy and depth. His results indicate that, as Barnes had already found, children's love of yellow diminishes with age; even between the ages of four and seven, though yellow was still one of the most favorite colors of the boys, it had ceased to be in any degree a favorite color with the girls. Lobsien, at Kiel, investigating the color preferences of a large number of school girls between the ages of eight and fourteen, reached congruent results; he adopted the method of offering the colors in pairs, and found that while orange was never preferred to any other color, there was a tendency at all ages to prefer yellow to green and usually to violet, but never to red or blue. These results harmonize with the conclusion of Garbini that in discrimination of color girls are more precocious than boys, though it must be added that, as in physical development, the period of adolescence brings to an end this greater rapidity of girls in development; thus Wissler, in comparing the color preferences of freshmen and seniors of both sexes, found (as Jastrow had previously found) that with age there is a shifting of preference towards the violet end of the spectrum which is the favorite end of men, red being that of women.

Investigations on students in various countries have almost invariably shown that yellow is the least attractive color. In Germany, Cohn found among students that yellow, even in any degree of saturation, was never the preferred color. In determining the color preferences of 100 students in Columbia University, it was found that yellow came, at a considerable distance, fourth, being only followed by green, while Wissler found that, for male and female students alike, yellow is of all colors the least frequently preferred (by two per cent, of the men and five per cent, of the women); among the men it was also the most frequently disliked, though among the women this dislike was transferred to orange. The dislike of female students to yellow, it will be seen, seems a little less marked than that of male students. This is confirmed by an inquiry at Wellesley

College, where it was found that though only 10 per cent, of the women preferred yellow, it was yet more frequently preferred than green or violet. At Cornell University, in a series of careful experiments on a small number of individuals, Major considered that there was no evidence of a positive dislike of yellow, yet all his subjects found yellow or orange among the least pleasant colors.

Among adults generally, it must be said finally, that yellow and orange are very seldom the favorite colors, and in ascertaining the color preferences of 4,500 men and women at the Chicago Exposition, Jastrow found that yellow and orange were the least preferred colors, though here also women seemed to like yellow more often than men.

But for mankind in general these results, undisputed as they probably are, do not hold universally good. There is one vast and highly important area of the world, by no means uncivilized in large part, where yellow, so far from being disparaged, is held in the highest honor. Throughout nearly the whole of Asia, ancient and modern—in Assyria, in India and in Ceylon, throughout China, in the Malay peninsula—yellow is usually the supreme and most sacred color. In India and Ceylon yellow is preferred, whether in flowers or in garments, and the substances that produce yellow dyes are held in highest honor and are essential in the ritual of many ceremonies; in the ceremonial of Hindu marriage, for instance, turmeric is always necessary. Turmeric is in India the substitute for the saffron, probably used by the Aryans be fore they reached India, which with its brilliant yellow as of the rising sun has been used by the men of many lands from the earliest ages. It was perhaps connected with sun-worship, as turmeric appears to be to-day in India. In Persia saffron possessed magic qualities and even in the medieval Europe saffron was worn in little bags and constantly used in the preparation of food. The Soma, it may be added, is of a golden color and is still used in Persia as a yellow dye. The Buddhists, again, hold yellow in highest honor, and the sacred flower of the Buddhists is yellow. In Persia, yellow is a favorite color, as it was with the Hebrews, for in the Song of Songs the bride is compared to saffron. In China, yellow is the fortunate color, though largely sharing this virtue with green and red. In the Malay states, white is holiest of all and is used to conciliate demons, but after white yellow is by far the most sacred color. According to Malay annals, a certain sultan prohibited the wearing of yellow garments in public, and even the use of yellow handkerchiefs or curtains, because yellow is too sacred for ordinary mortals, and ever since yellow has been the royal color in all Malay states. It may be added that on the western borders of

Asia, in ancient Egypt, although yellow was not the supreme color, it was still held in high honor; the favorite combination to express splendor was gold and lazuli.

Even in classic Europe, at the highest moments of the civilization we inherit today, yellow, though not occupying the sacred position it has always held in Asia, was yet a preferred color, always mentioned with an affective tone of delight. In both Greece and Rome — somewhat curiously, in view of what we have had to note of the psychic reaction to it in modern times — though red was the most sacred color, yellow was the color for the festival garments of women and children, and was especially worn,

Pliny states, by women at marriage. It was also the color of the priests of Cybele. Red and yellow, according to the same author, were the colors that dominated in ancient pictures. The four primary colors, according to Empedocles, are white, black, red and yellow, exactly the four colors which Nietzsche, discussing the philology of classic color-words, states that the Greek world seems to have been made of. Yellow was with red the favorite color of Homer, and Latin poetry is specially rich in synonyms for yellow.

What is the meaning of this clash of feeling between the modern European world, on the one side, and, on the other, the ancient classic world and the universal sentiments of Asia? It is not obvious why we should have ceased to delight in a color that to the men of another age and of another continent has seemed so precious, the color of the sun, of gold and of corn, of honey and of amber. It is still a very familiar color to us, alike in sunlight and artificial light, and when not too intense is in no degree fatiguing to the sense-organs; harmonious tones of yellow, indeed, in the scheme of the decoration of a room, are for many, perhaps for most, people highly agreeable to live in. Nor can we claim that our dislike to yellow reveals a more refined esthetic sensibility than the ancients possessed, for the painter knows nothing of this antipathy. In Rembrandt, indeed, we have a painter of the very highest rank who, as he slowly approached the culminating point of his art, was more and more fascinated by yellow, until in the end his pictures, even his portraits, are entirely covered by the shimmer of old gold.

It was clearly the advent of Christianity that introduced a new feeling in regard to yellow, leading, as Magnus has remarked, to a preference for the dark end of the spectrum. In very large measure, no doubt, this was merely the Outcome of the whole of the christian revulsion against the classic world and the rejection of everything which stood as the symbol of joy and pride. Red and yellow were the favorite colors of that world. The love of red was too firmly rooted in human nature for even Christianity to overcome it altogether, but yellow was a point of less resistance and here the new religion triumphed. Yellow became the color of envy.

In some measure, however, this feeling may have been not so much a reaction as the continuation of a natural development. The classic world had clearly begun, as savages have begun everywhere, with an almost exclusive delight in red, even an almost exclusive attention to it, and for Homer as for the Arabs the rainbow was predominantly red; yellow had next been added to the attractive colors; very slowly the other colors of the spectrum began to win attention. Thus Democritus substituted green for yellow in the list of primary colors previously given by Empedocles. It was at a comparatively late period that blue and violet became interesting or even acquired definite names. The invasion of Christianity happened in time to join in this movement along the spectrum — for even in the second century after Christ's birth Aulus Gellius when discussing colors scarcely mentions green and blue — and in doing so christian energy was reinforced by its instinctive repulsion for the brilliant colors associated with pagan rites and customs. Thus it was that not red or yellow, but blue, the hue of heaven, became the traditional color of the Virgin's raiment. In ecclesiastical usage yellow has never been regarded with favor; it has usually been either a color to avoid or to treat with indifference. This feeling has not diminished with the centuries; in 1833 the use of yellow in priests' garments was prohibited, and in the protestant church yellow has never been used at all.

Yellow became the color of jealousy, of envy, of treachery. Judas was painted in yellow garments and in some countries Jews were compelled to be so dressed. In France in the sixteenth century the doors of traitors and felons were daubed with yellow. In Spain heretics who recanted were enjoined to wear a yellow cross as a penance and the inquisition required them to appear at public *autos da fe* in penitential garments and carrying a yellow candle.

There is a special reason why Christianity should have viewed yellow with suspicion. It had been the color associated with wanton love. In the beginning the association was with legitimate love; it has already been noted that in classic times the bride's garments were yellow, while in the *Iliad* as well as in the Indian *Gitagovinda*, a bed of saffron is prepared for lovers. But in Greece, and to a still more marked extent in Rome, the courtezan began to take advantage of this association. The Greek hetaira and her Roman successor wore saffron-colored frocks and dyed their hair yellow. That professional custom of dyeing the hair has to some extent persisted, as we know, among their successors for more than two thousand years, throughout the middle ages to the present, and the injunction of Menander (as quoted by Clement of Alexandria), 'No chaste woman ought to make her hair yellow,' has been a perpetual refrain among the fathers of the church. It was as a reflection of the evolution of yellow in this direction that it became the symbolic color of inconstancy and adultery.

The outcome of the history of yellow during these two thousand years has been a curious opposition and contrast in the emotions it suggests. On the one hand, the affective tone of yellow in general has slowly become for most people either negatively indifferent or positively unpleasant. But the primitive and classic glorification of yellow has not absolutely died out. It has only concentrated itself around the word 'golden.' We see this mixed attitude reflected in the poets. They use the word 'yellow' with extreme parsimony as compared with their profuse employment of 'red,' but 'gold' and 'golden' constantly recur, and always with an emotional suggestion of beauty and splendor and joy. This is, for example, very marked in Keats. Even, however, in the use of 'golden,' it is still possible to trace a latent antipathy to the color yellow. In primitive times — among the Celtic makers of the Irish cycle of legends, for instance — it was the color quite as much as the preciousness of the metal that is felt to be desirable. But among our modern poets 'golden' has come very largely to mean what is beautiful or delightful, with little or no reference to color.

The epithet of 'golden-mouth,' which became the name of the eloquent Chrysostom, shows that 'gold' was used in a highly symbolic sense at an early period in the history of Christianity, while Shakespeare's 'golden lads and girls' is typical of this vague poetic use of the word. 'Golden' in English has largely come to mean not yellow or any other definite shade of color, but merely beautiful and precious, as 'red' means in Russia. The same contrast between 'yellow' and 'golden' may be found in other European languages; in French, for example, the affective tone of *jaune* is totally different from that of *or*, and it is the same in Italian and most other allied languages. As a general rule yellow is not applied by the poets to any object which suggests a definitely beautiful emotional tone, while 'golden' only in a minority of cases, as when applied to hair, corn, etc., bears any insistence on definite color.

It is not until the middle of the last century, at all events in England, that we find any definite revival of the old classic feeling in regard to yellow. It is very notable in Swinburne, who dwells with pleasure on honey and amber and other yellow substances, emphasizing their color; yet at the same time he usually avoids the use of the word yellow; 'white and gold and red,' he declares, are 'God's three chief words,' and he marks his sense of the inferiority of the word in the lines:

A comb of yellow shell for all the rest,
A comb of gold for the king's daughter.

In the course of centuries and until recent times, we find, there has thus been a gradually diminishing tendency to insist on the color of any beautiful or desirable object that is yellow. At the same time, there has been a tendency to emphasize the associations of yellow, which are really founded on one of the most ancient observations of man. Yellow is the color of bile and of a jaundiced skin. Most of the evil passions and impulses of mankind, in the popular science of primitive peoples, have their origin in the liver and the bile.

The degree to which mankind has been impressed by the yellowness of bile is sufficiently proved by the fact that bile has constantly served to supply a name to yellow; thus among the Eskimo, the Chukchis, the Samoyeds, the Voguls and other subarctic races yellow (and sometimes green) are called by a word which means bile. Even in our own Aryan tongues it seems to be the same, and 'gall' lies at the root not only of 'yellow' but also of 'green' and even of 'gold.' Hence it is that yellow is the color alike of envy and of melancholy.

We have in Shakespeare's phrase the 'jealous complexion' (orange) and 'green and yellow melancholy,' and in Pope the 'jaundiced eye' to which 'all seems yellow.' This perpetual inhibition, initiated by the early christians, of the agreeable associations of yellow, and the concomitant emphasis, not only in language but also in actual life, of all its most unpleasant associations, may possibly account for the predominant emotional tone of yellow among peoples of European origin today.

A doubt may indeed possibly arise as to the complete adequacy of such an explanation. Can we absolutely exclude any innate psychic tendency physiologically rooted in the organism? A curious circumstance recorded by Latta, in his careful psychological investigation of a man operated on at the age of thirty for congenital cataract, might possibly be held to support the doubt.

The first color that the subject noticed on recovering from the operation was red, while green took him the longest time to master. But 'the first time he saw yellow he became so sick that he thought he would vomit.' One might be tempted to regard this incident as a brilliant justification of the association between bile and yellow and of the attitude of Christendom towards this color; an adult man, whose visual sense-organs have retained their virginal delicacy, at once becomes 'bilious' when he sees yellow! But, even putting aside the possibility of idiosyncrasy, it is fairly obvious that the man would approach the sight of colors with certain prepossessions; we are not told that he was shown yellow without being informed of its name, and since blind people are interested and curious with regard to the nature of color, we may well believe that this man had imbibed the current ideas as to yellow and that the appropriate affective tone was already associated with the color before he had ever seen it.

However that may be, the strange history of yellow in the human mind and its striking vicissitudes are not only full of interest, but they really bring us up to a great problem which the psychologist must constantly face under a myriad of aspects: the respective parts which must be assigned to the innate properties of the psychic organism and to the temporary reactions it has acquired under the influence of a slowly shifting environment. How far, the psychologist must so often ask himself, am I investigating the intrinsic qualities of the stream of consciousness? How far am I registering the images reflected from its banks?

www.ingramcontent.com/pod-product-compliance
Lightning Source LLC
Chambersburg PA
CBHW051106250726

48656CB00001B/501